C.S.LEWIS

~ on ~

FAITH

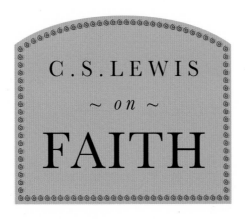

C. S. LEWIS

~ on ~

FAITH

Compiled by

LESLEY WALMSLEY

THOMAS NELSON PUBLISHERS
Nashville

Published in Nashville, Tennessee
by Thomas Nelson, Inc.

1 2 3 4 5 6 – 03 02 01 00 99 98

Extracts from C.S. Lewis's works © C.S. Lewis Pte Ltd.
Introduction and compilation © 1998 Lesley Walmsley
Cover illustration © 1998 Sarah Young

Produced for Thomas Nelson Inc. by Godsfield Press

Designed and produced by
THE BRIDGEWATER BOOK COMPANY LTD

Picture research by Jane Moore

The Catalog Card Number is on file
with the Library of Congress.

ISBN 0 7852 7095 7

Printed in Hong Kong

Contents

Introduction

'Faith' could be described as a strong or unshakeable belief in something, especially without proof or evidence. Everyone has faith in something or someone, even if it's just that the sun will rise tomorrow, or that your friend will meet you at the time and place appointed. But this selection from the writings of C.S. Lewis deals with a very specific form of faith, the Christian faith.

Clive Staples (Jack) Lewis was born in Belfast on 29 November 1898, and he and his brother Warren (Warnie) were brought up by their father, a member of the Church of Ireland, after their mother died. The boys took her death badly, seeing it as the act of a cruel God, and both grew up as atheists, a fact they tried to hide from their father.

Whilst Warnie pursued a career in the army, Jack's brilliant mind brought him academic success at Oxford. In 1923 he took a First in English Language and Literature, having already obtained Firsts in Classical Honour Moderations and Literae Humaniores, and two years later he was elected a Fellow of Magdalen College, where he was to spend most of his life.

His teaching brought him into daily contact with some of the finest minds of his generation, both other university lecturers and undergraduates, many of whom he was to influence for the rest of their lives. Some of the people he sparred with intellectually at

C.S. Lewis

Oxford were Christians, and eventually, in 1931, at the age of 32, and following his brother's example, C.S. Lewis 'gave in, and admitted that God was God... perhaps the most dejected and reluctant convert in all England'.

Oxford, from Headington Hill

*The Map of Narnia,
C.S. Lewis's make-believe world*

It was the combination of his lucid mind, and the inner struggles he had himself experienced, that made Jack Lewis so well able to express his own faith. His writings have had more influence on believers, both inside and outside the Christian Church, this century, than probably any other writer. Although he died in 1963 his works still go on speaking to people of all ages, both children – The Chronicles of Narnia *are among the most popular books for children published this century – and adults.*

Lewis's books – Mere Christianity, Miracles, The Problem of Pain, The Four Loves, The Abolition of Man, Reflections on the Psalms, The Great Divorce, Surprised by Joy, Prayer – Letters to Malcolm, *to name but a few – present Christian beliefs in a way that no one else has ever done. Lewis had been compelled to think everything through for himself, and he accepted nothing handed down from someone else. He had to struggle with*

what he had written, and he was therefore quite clear in his own mind about what he believed on any subject. But when he was still thinking something through, he admitted it. To anyone seeking belief, here was someone who had already trudged the way, and who had earned the right to say 'This is what I believe'. (Though Lewis never said, 'And therefore so should you'.) He wanted to help others to find their own faith, knowing that saying 'This is the truth. Accept it' had not worked for him and probably would not for them.

'The Inklings'

C.S. Lewis was writing in a very different world from the one in which we live today. In particular, women at that time were only beginning to exert much of an influence outside the home, and it was quite normal to refer to 'a man who', whereas today we would more naturally use inclusive language. Lewis respected everyone for what they were, and if he were writing now I am sure that this would be reflected in his style. But he is not, and I have decided to leave his thoughts exactly as he expressed them.

This book will give you some idea of the mind and belief of C.S. Lewis. I hope that this selection from the amazingly rich treasury of his faith will encourage you to read the actual books for yourself.

≈ LESLEY WALMSLEY

The First Day of Creation,
JULIUS SCHNORR VON CAROLSFIELD (1794–1874)

Christian belief

I have been asked to tell you what Christians believe, and I am going to begin by telling you one thing that Christians do not need to believe. If you are an atheist you do have to believe that the main point in all the religions of the whole world is simply one huge mistake. If you are a Christian you do not have to believe that all the other religions are simply wrong all through. ... If you are a Christian, you are free to think that all those religions, even the queerest ones, contain at least some hint of the truth... But, of course, being a Christian does mean thinking that where Christianity differs from other religions, Christianity is right and they are wrong. As in arithmetic – there is only one right answer to a sum, and all other answers are wrong; but some of the wrong answers are much nearer being right than others.

≈ *MERE CHRISTIANITY*

Gift-love and Need-love

'God is love,' says St John ... I thought that his maxim would provide me with a very plain highroad through the whole subject ... The first distinction I made was therefore between what I called Gift-love and Need-love. The typical example of Gift-love would be that love which moves a man to work and plan and save for the future well-being of his family  which he will die without sharing or seeing; of the second, that which sends a lonely or frightened child to its mother's arms.

There was no doubt which was more like Love Himself. Divine Love is Gift-love. The Father gives all He is and has to the Son. The Son gives Himself back to the Father, and gives Himself to the world, and for the world to the Father, and thus gives the world (in Himself) back to the Father too.

≈ *THE FOUR LOVES*

The word 'Christian'

Now if once we allow people to start spiritualizing and refining, or as they might say 'deepening', the sense of the word *Christian,* it too will speedily become a useless word. In the first place, Christians themselves will never be able to apply it to anyone. It is not for us to say who, in the deepest sense, is or is not close to the spirit of Christ. We do not see into men's hearts. We cannot judge, and are indeed forbidden to judge. It would be wicked arrogance for us to say that any man is, or is not, a Christian in this refined sense. And obviously a word which we can never apply is not going to be a very useful word. As for the unbelievers, they will no doubt cheerfully use the word in the refined sense. It will become in their mouths simply a term of praise. In calling anyone a Christian they will mean that they think him a good man. But that way of using the word will be no enrichment of the language, for we already have the word *good.* Meanwhile, the word *Christian* will have been spoiled for any really useful purpose it might have served.

We must, therefore stick to the original, obvious

meaning. The name *Christians* was first given at Antioch (Acts 11:26) to 'the disciples', to those who accepted the teaching of the apostles. There is no question of its being restricted to those who profited by that teaching as much as they should have. There is no question of its being extended to those who in some refined, spiritual, inward fashion were 'far closer to the spirit of Christ' than the less satisfactory of the disciples. The point is not a theological or moral one. It is only a question of using words so that we can all understand what is being said. When a man who accepts the Christian doctrine lives unworthily of it, it is much clearer to say he is a bad Christian than to say he is not a Christian.

≈ *MERE CHRISTIANITY*

The Birth of Christ (detail), BOTTICELLI (1445–1510)

'Why do you not believe in God?'

When I was an atheist ... there was one question which I never dreamed of raising. ... If the universe is so bad, or even half so bad, how on earth did human beings ever come to attribute it to the activity of a wise and good Creator? ... The spectacle of the universe as revealed by experience can never have been the ground of religion; it must always have been something in spite of which religion, acquired from a different source, was held...

In all developed religion we find three strands or elements, and in Christianity one more. The first of these is... the *Numinous*... (which) is not the same as the morally good, and a man overwhelmed with awe is likely, if left to himself, to think the numinous object 'beyond good and evil'. This brings us to the second strand or element in religion. All human beings... acknowledge some kind of morality; that is, they feel towards certain proposed actions the experiences expressed by the words 'I ought' or 'I ought not'. ... The

third stage in religious development arises when men identify them – when the Numinous Power to which they feel awe is made the guardian of the morality to which they feel obligation... The fourth strand or element is a historical event. There was a man born among (these) Jews who claimed to be, or to be the son of, or to be 'one with', the Something which is at once the awful haunter of nature and the giver of the moral law. The claim is so shocking... that only two views of this man are possible. Either He was a raving lunatic of an unusually abominable type, or else He was, and is, precisely what He said.

≈ *THE PROBLEM OF PAIN*

The Narrow Gate to Heaven and the Wide Gate to Hell,
CORNELIS DE BIE (1621–54)

The reluctant convert

You must picture me alone in that room at Magdalen, night after night, feeling, whenever my mind lifted even for a second from my work, the steady, unrelenting approach of Him whom I so earnestly

desired not to meet. That which I greatly feared had at last come upon me. In the Trinity Term of 1929 I gave in, admitted that God was God, and knelt and prayed: perhaps, that night, the most dejected and reluctant convert in all England...

Magdalen College,
Oxford

The conversion ... was only to theism, pure and simple, not to Christianity. I knew nothing yet about the Incarnation. The God to whom I surrendered was sheerly non-human... My conversion involved as yet no belief in a future life. I now number it among my greatest mercies that I was permitted for several months, perhaps for a year, to know God and to attempt obedience without even raising that question...

I know very well when, but hardly how, the final step was taken. I was driven to Whipsnade one sunny morning. When we set out I did not believe that Jesus Christ is the Son of God, and when we reached the zoo I did.

≈ *SURPRISED BY JOY*

Questions that divide

Martin Luther at the Reichstag in Worms,
PAUL THUMANN (1834–1908)

In the first place, the questions which divide Christians from one another often involve points of high theology or even of ecclesiastical history, which ought never to be treated except by real experts. I should have been out of my depth in such waters: more in need of help myself than able to help others. And secondly, I think we must admit that the discussion of these disputed

points has no tendency at all to bring an outsider into the Christian fold. So long as we write and talk about them we are much more likely to deter him from entering any Christian communion than to draw him into our own. ... Finally, I got the impression that far more, and more talented, authors were already engaged in such controversial matters than in the defence of what Baxter calls 'mere' Christianity. That part of the line where I thought I could serve best was also the part that seemed to be thinnest. And to it I naturally went...

Certainly I have met with little of the fabled *odium theologicum* from convinced members of communions different from my own. Hostility has come more from borderline people. ... men not exactly obedient to any communion. This I find curiously consoling. It is at her centre, where her truest children dwell, that each communion is really closest to every other in spirit, if not in doctrine. And this suggests that at the centre of each there is a something, or a Someone, who against all divergencies of belief, all differences of temperament, all memories of mutual persecution, speaks with the same voice.

≈ *MERE CHRISTIANITY*

A place to wait in

'Mere' Christianity... is... like a hall out of which doors open into several rooms. If I can bring anyone into that hall I shall have done what I attempted. But it is in the rooms, not in the hall, that there are fires and chairs and meals. The hall is a place to wait in, a place from which to try the various doors, not a place to live in. For that purpose the worst of the rooms (whichever that may be) is, I think, preferable. It is true that some people may find they have to wait in the hall for a considerable time, while others feel certain almost at once which door they must knock at. I do not know why there is this difference, but I am sure God keeps no one waiting unless He sees that it is good for him to wait...

When you do get into your room you will find that the long wait has done you some kind of good which you would not have had otherwise. But you must regard it as waiting, not as camping. You must keep on praying for light: and, of course, even in the hall, you must begin trying to obey the rules which are common to the whole house. And above all you must be asking which door is

the true one; not which pleases you best by its paint and panelling…

When you have reached your own room, be kind to those who have chosen different doors and to those who are still in the hall. If they are wrong they need your prayers all the more; and if they are your enemies, then you are under orders to pray for them. That is one of the rules common to the whole house.

≈ *MERE CHRISTIANITY*

Illustration from *Jerusalem,* WILLIAM BLAKE (1757–1827)

He makes
each soul unique

'I reckon,' said St Paul, 'that the sufferings of this present time are not worthy to be compared with the glory that shall be revealed in us' (Romans 8:18)... We are very shy nowadays of even mentioning heaven. We are afraid of the jeer about 'pie in the sky', and of being told that we are trying to 'escape' from the duty of making a happy world here and now into dreams of a happy world elsewhere. But either there is 'pie in the sky' or there is not. If there is not, then Christianity is false, for this doctrine is woven into its whole fabric. If there is, then this truth, like any other, must be faced...

Again, we are afraid that heaven is a bribe, and that if we make it our goal we shall no longer be disinterested. It is not so. Heaven offers nothing that a mercenary soul can desire. It is safe to tell the pure in heart that they shall see God, for only the pure in heart want to. There are rewards that do not sully motives. Love, by definition, seeks to enjoy its object...

I am considering not how, but why, He makes each soul unique. If He had no use for all these differences, I do not see why He should have created more souls than one. Be sure that the ins and outs of your individuality are no mystery to Him; and one day they will no longer be a mystery to you... Your soul has a curious shape because it is a hollow made to fit a particular swelling in the infinite contours of the Divine substance, or a key to unlock one of the doors in the house with many mansions. For it is not humanity in the abstract that is to be saved, but you – you, the individual reader... Your place in heaven will seem

The Wrath of Elihu from *The Book of Job*, WILLIAM BLAKE (1757–1827)

to be made for you and you alone, because you were made for it – made for it stitch by stitch as a glove is made for a hand.

≈ *THE PROBLEM OF PAIN*

[23]

What is good or bad?

The Deposition of Christ, GIOTTO (1266–1337)

If you do not take the distinction between good and bad very seriously, then it is easy to say that anything you find in this world is a part of God. But, of course, if you think some things really bad, and God really good, then you cannot talk like that. You must believe that God is separate from the world and that some of the things we see in it are contrary to His will... Christianity... thinks God made the world... But it also thinks that a great many things have gone wrong with the world that God made and that God insists, and insists very loudly, on our putting them right again... And, of course, that raises a very big question. If a good God made the world why has it gone wrong? ...

And for many years... my argument against God was that the universe seemed so cruel and unjust. But how had I got this idea of *just* and *unjust?* A man does not call a line crooked unless he has some idea of a straight line. What was I comparing this universe with when I called it unjust? If the whole show was bad and senseless from A to Z, so to speak, why did I, who was supposed to be part of the show, find myself in such violent reaction against it?... Thus in the very act of trying to prove that God did not exist – in other words, that the whole of reality was senseless – I found I was forced to assume that one part of reality – namely my idea of justice – was full of sense. Consequently atheism turns out to be too simple. If the whole universe has no meaning, we should never have found out that it has no meaning: just as, if there were no light in the universe and therefore no creatures with eyes, we should never know it was dark. *Dark* would be a word without meaning.

≈ *MERE CHRISTIANITY*

An intuition of God

It is clear that there never was a time when nothing existed; otherwise nothing would exist now. But to exist means to be a positive Something, to have (metaphorically) a certain shape... The Thing which always existed, namely God, has therefore always had His own positive character...

Why, then, do the mystics talk of Him as they do, and why are many people prepared in advance to maintain that, whatever else God may be, He is not the concrete, living, willing, and acting God of Christian theology? I think the reason is as follows. Let us suppose a mystical limpet, a sage among limpets, who (rapt in vision) catches a glimpse of what Man is like. In reporting it to his disciples... he will have to use many negatives. He will have to tell them that Man has no shell, is not attached to a rock, is not surrounded by water. And his disciples, having little vision of their own to help them, do get some idea of Man. But then there come erudite limpets, limpets who write histories of philosophy and give lectures on comparative religion, and who have never had any vision of their own. What they get out of

God the Father Enthroned, JACOPO ALBEREGNO (D.1397)

the prophetic limpet's words is simply and solely the negatives. From these… they build up a picture of Man as a sort of amorphous jelly (he has no shell) existing nowhere in particular (he is not attached to a rock) and never taking nourishment (there is no water to drift it towards him)…

Our own situation is much like that of the erudite limpets… At each step we have to strip off from our idea of God some human attribute. But the only real reason for stripping off the human attribute is to make room for putting in some positive divine attribute. In St Paul's language, the purpose of all this unclothing is not that our idea of God should reach nakedness but that it should be re-clothed.

≈ *MIRACLES*

'I am the Lord'

We who defend Christianity find ourselves constantly opposed not by the irreligion of our hearers but by their real religion. Speak about beauty, truth and goodness, or about a God who is simply the indwelling principle of these three, speak about a great spiritual force pervading all things, a common mind of which we are all parts, a pool of generalized spirituality to which we can all flow, and you will command friendly interest. But the temperature drops as soon as you mention a God... with a determinate character...

Let us dare to say that God... is 'absolute being' – or rather *the* Absolute Being... He is righteous, not a-moral; creative, not inert. The Hebrew writings here observe an admirable balance. Once God says simply I AM, proclaiming the mystery of self-existence. But times without number He says 'I am the Lord'... And men are exhorted to 'know the Lord', to discover and experience this particular character.

≈ *MIRACLES*

Illustration from *Europe: A Prophecy*, WILLIAM BLAKE (1757–1827)

King David with Musicians
8TH-CENTURY ANGLO-SAXON
ILLUMINATED MANUSCRIPT

The poetry of God

The Psalms are poems, and poems intended to be sung: not doctrinal treatises, nor even sermons. Their chief formal characteristic, the most obvious element of pattern, is... the practice of saying the same thing twice in different words. A perfect example is... 'He shall make thy righteousness as clear as the light; and thy just dealing as the noonday' (Psalms 37:6). If we have any taste for poetry we shall enjoy this feature of the Psalms. Even those Christians who cannot enjoy it will respect it; for Our Lord, soaked in the poetic tradition of His country, delighted to use it. 'For with what judgement ye judge, ye shall be judged; and with what measure ye mete, it shall be measured to you again ...' (Matthew 7:2)

It seems to me appropriate, almost inevitable, that when that great Imagination which in the beginning, for Its own delight and for the delight of men and angels and (in their proper mode) of beasts, had invented and formed the whole world of Nature, submitted to express Itself in human speech, that speech should sometimes be poetry. For poetry too is a little incarnation, giving body to what had been before invisible and inaudible.

≈ *REFLECTIONS ON THE PSALMS*

The Way which every man should tread

St Augustine defines virtue as *ordo amoris*, the ordinate condition of the affections in which every object is accorded that kind and degree of love which is appropriate to it. Aristotle says that the aim of education is to make the pupil like and dislike what he ought. When the age of reflective thought comes, the pupil who has been thus trained in 'ordinate affections' or 'just sentiments' will easily find the first principles in Ethics; but to the corrupt man they will never be visible at all and he can make no progress in that science...

The Chinese also speak of a great thing (the greatest thing) called the *Tao*. It is the reality beyond all predicates, the abyss that was before the Creator Himself... It is also the Way which every man should tread in imitation of that cosmic and supercosmic progression, conforming all activities to that great exemplar...

The educational problem is wholly different according as you stand within or without the *Tao*. For those within, the task is to train in the pupil those responses which are in themselves appropriate, whether anyone is making them or not, and in making which the very nature of man consists. Those without, if they are logical, must regard all sentiments as equally non-rational, as mere mists between us and the real objects. As a result, they must either decide to remove all sentiments, as far as possible, from the pupil's mind; or else to encourage some sentiments for reasons that have nothing to do with their intrinsic 'justness' or 'ordinacy'...

And all the time ... we continue to clamour for those very qualities we are rendering impossible. You can hardly open a periodical without coming across the statement that what our civilization needs is more 'drive', or dynamism, or self-sacrifice, or 'creativity'. In a sort of ghastly simplicity we remove the organ and demand the function... We laugh at honour and are shocked to find traitors in our midst. We castrate and bid the geldings be fruitful.

≈ *THE ABOLITION OF MAN*

A part of Heaven itself

Blake wrote *The Marriage of Heaven and Hell*. If I have written of their Divorce, this is not because I think myself a fit antagonist for so great a genius, nor even because I feel at all sure that I know what he meant. But in some sense or other the attempt to make that marriage is perennial. The attempt is based on the belief that reality never presents us with an absolutely unavoidable 'either-or'; that, granted skill and patience and (above all) time enough, some way of embracing both alternatives can always be found; that mere development or adjustment or refinement will somehow turn evil into good without our being called on for a final and total rejection of anything we should like to retain. This belief I take to be a disastrous error...

We are not living in a world where all roads are radii of a circle and where all, if followed long enough, will therefore draw gradually nearer and finally meet at the centre: rather in a world where every road, after a

few miles, forks into two, and each of those into two again, and at each fork you must make a decision... Good, as it ripens, becomes continually more different not only from evil but from other good...

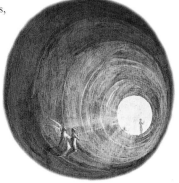

I believe, to be sure, that any man who reaches Heaven will find... that the kernel of what he was really seeking even in his most depraved wishes will be there, beyond expectation... But we, at this end of the road, must not try to

The Ascent to the Heavenly Paradisee,
HIERONYMUS BOSCH (1450-1516)

anticipate that retrospective vision. If we do, we are likely to embrace the false and disastrous converse and fancy that everything is good and everywhere is Heaven...

Earth, I think, will not be found by anyone to be in the end a very distinct place. I think earth, if chosen instead of heaven, will turn out to have been, all along, only a region in Hell: and earth, if put second to heaven, to have been from the beginning a part of heaven itself.

≈ *THE GREAT DIVORCE*

The Devil
as Screwtape

There are two equal and opposite errors into which our race can fall about the devils. One is to disbelieve in their existence. The other is to believe, and to feel an excessive and unhealthy interest in them...

The proper question is whether I believe in devils. I do. That is to say, I believe in angels and I believe that some of these, by the abuse of their free will, have become enemies to God and, as a corollary, to us. These we may call devils. They do not differ in nature from good angels, but their nature is depraved. *Devil* is the opposite of *angel* only as Bad Man is the opposite

Job's Sons and Daughters Destroyed from *The Book of Job*, WILLIAM BLAKE (1757–1827)

of Good Man. Satan, the leader or dictator of devils, is the opposite not of God but of Michael...

I live in the Managerial Age, in a world of 'Admin'. The greatest evil is not now done in those sordid 'dens of crime' that Dickens loved to paint... It is conceived and ordered... in clean, carpeted, warmed and well-lighted offices, by quiet men with white collars and cut fingernails and smooth-shaven cheeks who do not need to raise their voice. Hence, naturally enough, my symbol for Hell is something like the bureaucracy of a police state or the offices of a thoroughly nasty business concern...

(As Screwtape wrote): It does not matter how small the sins are provided that their cumulative effect is to edge the man away from the Light and out into the Nothing... Indeed the safest road to Hell is the gradual one – the gentle slope, soft underfoot, without sudden turnings, without milestones, without signposts.

≈ *THE SCREWTAPE LETTERS*

Pride

I now come to that part of Christian morals where they differ most sharply from all other morals. There is one vice of which no man in the world is free; which everyone in the world loathes when he sees it in someone else; and of which hardly any people, except Christians, ever imagine that they are guilty themselves… The vice I am talking of is Pride or Self-conceit: and the virtue opposite to it, in Christian morals, is called Humility…

Fallen Angel, ODILON REDON (1840–1916)

According to Christian teachers, the essential vice, the utmost evil, is Pride. Unchastity, anger, greed, drunkenness, and all that, are mere flea-bites in comparison: it was through Pride that the devil became the devil: Pride leads to every other vice: it is the complete anti-God state of mind...

Pride gets no pleasure out of having something, only out of having more of it than the next man... It is the comparison that makes you proud: the pleasure of being above the rest. Once the element of competition has gone, Pride has gone. That is why I say that Pride is essentially competitive in a way the other vices are not... Greed may drive men into competition if there is not enough to go round; but the proud man, even when he has got more than he can possibly want, will try to get still more just to assert his power. Nearly all those evils in the world which people put down to greed or selfishness are really far more the result of Pride.

≈ *MERE CHRISTIANITY*

The Fall of Man

According to the doctrine of the Fall, man is now a horror to God and to himself, and a creature ill-adapted to the universe not because God made him so but because he has made himself so by the abuse of his free will. To my mind this is the sole function of the doctrine. It exists to guard against two sub-Christian theories of the origin of evil – Monism, according to which God Himself, being 'above good and evil', produced impartially the effects to which we give those two names, and Dualism, according to which God produces good, while some equal and independent power produces evil. Against both these views Christianity asserts that God is good; that He made all things good for the sake of their goodness; that one of the good things He made, namely, the free will of rational creatures, by its very nature included the possibility of evil; and that creatures, availing themselves of this possibility, have become evil.

≈ *THE PROBLEM OF PAIN*

Equality

I am a democrat because I believe in the Fall of Man. I think most people are democrats for the opposite reason. A great deal of democratic enthusiasm descends from the ideas of people like Rousseau, who believed in democracy because they thought mankind so wise and good that everyone deserved a share in the government. The danger of defending democracy on those grounds is that they're not true. And whenever their weakness is exposed, the people who prefer tyranny make capital out of the exposure. I find that they're not true without looking further than myself. I don't deserve a share in governing a hen roost, much less a nation. Nor do most people – all the people who believe advertisements, and think in catchwords and spread rumours. The real reason for democracy is just the reverse. Mankind is so fallen that no man can be trusted with unchecked power over his fellows.

≈ 'EQUALITY'

Hell

It has been admitted... that man has free will and that all gifts to him are therefore two-edged. From these premises it follows directly that the Divine labour to redeem the world cannot be certain of succeeding as regards every individual soul. Some will not be redeemed... If the happiness of a creature lies in self-surrender, no one can make that surrender but himself (though many can help him to make it) and he may refuse...

I would pay any price to be able to say truthfully 'All will be saved'. But my reason retorts, 'Without their will, or with it?' If I say, 'Without their will' I at once perceive a contradiction; how can the supreme voluntary act of self-surrender be involuntary? If I say 'With their will', my reason replies 'How if they *will not* give in?' ...

The Dominical utterances about Hell... are addressed to the conscience and the will, not to our intellectual curiosity. When they have roused us into action by convincing us of a terrible possibility, they have done, probably, all they were intended to do; and if all the world were convinced Christians it would be unnecessary to say a word more on the subject. As things are, however, this doctrine is one of the chief grounds on which Christianity is attacked as barbarous, and the goodness of God impugned. We are... reminded of the tragedies in human life which have come from believing it. Of the other tragedies which come from not believing it we are told less. For these reasons, and these alone, it becomes necessary to discuss the matter.

≈ *THE PROBLEM OF PAIN*

God will be
guiding me

I may always feel looking back on any past sin that in the very heart of my evil passion there was something that God approves and wants me to feel not less but more. Take a sin of lust. The overwhelming thirst for rapture was good and even divine: it has not got to be unsaid (so to speak) and recanted. But it will never be quenched as I tried to quench it. If I refrain… God will be guiding me as quickly as He can to where I shall get what I really wanted all the time. It will not be very like what I now think I want: but it will be more like it than some suppose. In any case it will be the real thing, not a consolation prize or substitute. If I had it I should not need to fight against sensuality as something impure: rather I should spontaneously turn away from it as something dull, cold, abstract and artificial…

When we are tempted, we must remember that *just because* God wants for us what we really want and knows the only way to get it, therefore He must, in a sense, be quite ruthless towards sin…. The more He loves you the

more determined He must be to pull you back from your way which leads nowhere, into His way which leads you where you want to go... You may go the wrong way again, and again He may forgive you... But there is no hope *in the end* of getting where you want to go except by going God's way...

If endless time will really help us to go the right way, I believe we shall be given endless time. But perhaps God knows that time makes no difference. Perhaps He knows that if you can't learn the way in 60 or 70 years... then you will never learn it... There may be nothing left for Him but to destroy you (the kindest thing): *if He can.*

≈ *THEY STAND TOGETHER*

The Novices Searching for their Souls
SIMON PALMER (B.1956)

Miracles

The question whether miracles occur can never be answered simply by experience. Every event which might claim to be a miracle is, in the last resort, something presented to our senses, something seen, heard, touched, smelled, or tasted. And our senses are not infallible. If anything extraordinary seems to have happened, we can always say that we have been the victims of an illusion. If we hold a philosophy which excludes the supernatural, this is what we always shall say. What we learn from experience depends on the kind of philosophy we bring to experience...

Many people think one can decide whether a miracle occurred in the past by examining the evidence 'according to the ordinary rules of

The Angels Make their Beds and the Feathers Fly Down, JULIUS KLEINMICHEL (1846–92)

historical enquiry'. But the ordinary rules cannot be worked until we have decided whether miracles are possible, and if so, how probable they are. For if they are impossible, then no amount of historical evidence will convince us. If they are possible but immensely improbable, then only mathematically demonstrative evidence will convince us: and since history never provides that degree of evidence for any event, history can never convince us that a miracle occurred. If, on the other hand, miracles are not intrinsically improbable, then the existing evidence will be sufficient to convince us that quite a number of miracles have occurred…

It is no use going to the texts until we have some idea about the possibility or probability of the miraculous. Those who assume that miracles cannot happen are merely wasting their time by looking into the texts: we know in advance what results they will find for they have begun by begging the question.

≈ *MIRACLES*

The Grand Miracle

The central miracle asserted by Christians is the Incarnation. They say that God became Man. Every other miracle prepares for this, or results from this. Just as every natural event is the manifestation at a particular place and moment of Nature's total character, so every particular Christian miracle manifests at a particular place and moment the character and significance of the Incarnation. There is no question in Christianity of arbitrary interferences just scattered about. It relates not a series of disconnected raids on Nature but the various steps of a strategically coherent invasion – an invasion which intends complete conquest and 'occupation'. The fitness, and therefore credibility, of the particular miracles depends on their relation to the Grand Miracle; all discussion of them in isolation from it is futile...

The fitness or credibility of the Grand Miracle itself cannot, obviously, be judged by the same standard. And let us admit at once that it is very difficult to find a standard by which it can be judged. If the thing happened, it was the central event in the history of the Earth – the very thing that the whole story has been about. Since it happened only once, it is by Hume's standards infinitely improbable. But then the whole history of the Earth has also happened only once; is it therefore incredible?...

The historical difficulty of giving for the life, sayings and influence of Jesus any explanation that is not harder than the Christian explanation, is very great. The discrepancy between the depth and sanity and (let me add) *shrewdness* of His moral teaching and the rampant megalomania which must lie behind His theological teaching unless He is indeed God, has never been satisfactorily got over.

≈ *MIRACLES*

The Last Judgement (detail), FRA ANGELICO (C.1400–1455)

The highest
of the virtues

If you asked twenty good men today what they thought the highest of the virtues, nineteen of them would reply, Unselfishness. But if you had asked almost any of the great Christians of old he would have replied, Love. You see what has happened? A negative term has been substituted for a positive, and this is of more than philological importance. The negative idea of unselfishness carries with it the suggestion not primarily of securing good things for others, but of going without

them ourselves, as if our abstinence and not their happiness was the important point. I do not think this is the Christian virtue of Love.

The New Testament has lots to say about self-denial, but not about self-denial as an end in itself. We are told to deny ourselves and to take up our crosses in order that we may follow Christ; and nearly every description of what we shall ultimately find if we do so contains an appeal to desire. If there lurks in most modern minds the notion that to desire our own good and earnestly to hope for the enjoyement of it is a bad thing, I submit that this notion has crept in from Kant and the Stoics and is no part of the Christian faith. Indeed, if we consider the unblushing promises of reward and the staggering nature of the rewards promised in the gospels, it would seem that Our Lord finds our desires, not too strong, but too weak. We are half-hearted creatures, fooling about with drink and sex and ambition when infinite joy is offered us, like an ignorant child who wants to go on making mud pies in a slum because he cannot imagine what is meant by the offer of a holiday at the sea. We are far too easily pleased.

≈ 'THE WEIGHT OF GLORY'

The art of worship

It is probably true that a new, keen vicar will usually be able to form within his parish a minority who are in favour of his innovations. The majority, I believe, never are. Is this simply because the majority are hidebound? I think not. They have a good reason for their conservatism. Novelty, simply as such, can have only an entertainment value. And they don't go to church to be entertained. They go to *use* the service, or, if you prefer, to *enact* it.

Every service is a structure of acts and words through which we receive a sacrament, or repent, or supplicate, or adore. And it enables us to do these things best – if you like, it 'works' best – when, through long familiarity, we don't have to think about it. As long as you notice, and have to count, the steps, you are not yet dancing but only learning to dance. A good shoe is a shoe you don't notice. The perfect church service would be one we were almost unaware of; our attention would have been on God...

My whole liturgiological position really boils down to an entreaty for permanence and uniformity. I can make do with almost any kind of service whatever, if only it will stay put. But if each form is snatched away just when I am beginning to feel at home in it, then I can never make any progress in the art of worship.

≈ *PRAYER: LETTERS TO MALCOLM*

The Last Supper (detail) ANDREA DEL CASTAGNO (1423–1457)

Allegory and myth

What I meant by 'Romanticism' when I wrote *The Pilgrim's* was… a particular recurrent experience which dominated my childhood and adolescence and which I hastily called 'Romantic' because inanimate nature and marvellous literature were among the things

C.S. Lewis

that evoked it. I still believe that the experience is common, commonly misunderstood, and of immense importance: but I now know… that to bring it into the forefront of consciousness is not so easy as I once supposed…

To supply a 'key' to an allegory may encourage that particular misunderstanding of allegory which, as a literary critic, I have elsewhere denounced. It may encourage people to suppose that allegory is a disguise, a way of saying obscurely what could have been said more clearly. But in fact all good allegory exists not to hide but to reveal; to make the inner world more palpable by giving it an (imagined)

concrete embodiment… It remains true that wherever the symbols are best, the key is least adequate. For when allegory is at its best, it approaches myth, which must be grasped with the imagination, not with the intellect. If, as I still sometimes hope, my North and South and my Mr Sensible have some touch of mythical life, then no amount of 'explanation' will quite catch up with their meaning. It is the sort of thing you cannot learn from definition: you must rather get to know it as you get to know a smell or a taste, the 'atmosphere' of a family or a country town, or the personality of an individual.

≈ *THE PILGRIM'S REGRESS*

The God Thor Chasing the Dwarfs, RICHARD DOYLE (1824–83)

Job's Sacrifice from *The Book of Job*, WILLIAM BLAKE (1757–1827)

Does prayer work?

What sort of evidence would prove the efficacy of prayer? The thing we pray for may happen, but how can you ever know it was not going to happen anyway? The answer surely is that a compulsive empirical proof such as we have in the sciences can never be attained.

Now even if all the things that people prayed for happened, which they do not, this would not prove what Christians mean by the efficacy of prayer. For prayer is request. The essence of request, as distinct from compulsion, is that it may or may not be granted. And if

an infinitely wise Being listens to the requests of finite
and foolish creatures, of course He will sometimes grant
and sometimes refuse them...

There are, no doubt, passages in the New Testament
which may seem at first sight to promise an invariable
granting of our prayers. But that cannot be what they
really mean. For in the very heart of the story we meet a
glaring instance to the contrary. In Gethsemane the
holiest of all petitioners prayed three times that a certain
cup might pass from Him. It did not. After that the idea
that prayer is recommended to us as a sort of infallible
gimmick may be dismissed...

It is not really stranger, nor less strange, that my
prayers should affect the course of events than that my
other actions should do so. They have not advised or
changed God's mind – that is, His overall purpose. But
that purpose will be realized in different ways according
to the actions, including the prayers, of His creatures...
Prayer is not a machine. It is not magic... Our act,
when we pray, must not, any more than all our other
acts, be separated from the continuous act of God
Himself, in which alone all finite causes operate.

≈ 'THE EFFICACY OF PRAYER'

God is Love

G od is love. Again, 'Herein is love, not that we loved God but that He loved us' (1 John 4:10). We must not begin with mysticism, with the creature's love for God, or with the wonderful foretastes of the fruition of God vouchsafed to some in their earthly life. We begin at the real beginning, with love as the Divine energy. This primal love is Gift-love. In God there is no hunger that needs to be filled, only plenteousness that desires to give...

The doctrine that God was under no necessity to create is not a piece of dry scholastic speculation. It is essential. Without it we can hardly avoid the conception of what I can only call a 'managerial' God; a Being whose function or nature is to 'run' the universe, who stands to it as a headmaster to a school or a hotelier to a hotel. But to be sovereign of the universe is no great matter to God. In Himself, at home in 'the land of the Trinity', He is sovereign of a far greater realm. We must keep always before our eyes that vision of Lady Julian's in which God carried in His hand a little object like a nut, and that nut was 'all that is made'…

But in addition to these natural loves God can bestow a far better gift; or rather, since our minds must divide and pigeonhole, two gifts… He communicates to men a share of His own Gift-love… and a supernatural Need-love of Himself and a supernatural Need-love of one another.

≈ *THE FOUR LOVES*

Appreciative
Love of God

'Is it easy to love God?' asks an old author. 'It is easy,' he replies, 'to those who do it.' I have included two Graces (Gift-love and Need-love of God) under the word *Charity*. But God can give a third. He can awake in man, towards Himself, a supernatural Appreciative Love. This is of all gifts the most to be desired. Here, not in our natural loves... lies the true centre of all human and angelic life. With this all things are possible...

Perhaps, for many of us all experience merely defines, so to speak, the shape of that gap where our love of God ought to be. It is not enough. It is something. If we cannot 'practise the presence of God', it is something to practise the absence of God, to become increasingly aware of our unawareness till we feel like men who should stand beside a great cataract and hear no noise, or like a man in a story who looks in a mirror and finds no face there, or a man in a dream who stretches out his hand to visible objects and gets no sensation of touch. To know that one is dreaming is to be no longer perfectly asleep.

≈ *THE FOUR LOVES*

Dawn,
MAURICE DENIS (1870–1943)

To love is to
be vulnerable

In words which can still bring tears to the eyes, St Augustine describes the desolation in which the death of his friend Nebridius plunged him (*Confessions* IV, 10). Then he draws a moral. This is what comes, he says, of giving one's heart to anything but God. All human beings pass away. Do not let your happiness depend on something you may lose. If love is to be a blessing, not a misery, it must be for the only Beloved who will never pass away.

Of course this is excellent sense... Of all arguments against love none makes so strong an appeal to my nature as 'Careful! This might lead you to suffering.'

To my nature, my temperament, yes. Not to my conscience. When I respond to that appeal I seem to myself to be a thousand miles away from Christ. If I am sure of anything I am sure that His teaching was never meant to confirm my congenital preference for safe investments and limited liabilities. I doubt whether there is anything in me that pleases Him less. And who could conceivably begin to love God on such a prudential

ground – because the security (so to speak) is better? Who could even include it among the grounds for loving?... One must be outside the world of love, of all loves, before one thus calculates....

There is no escape along the lines St Augustine suggests... To love at all is to be vulnerable. Love anything, and your heart will certainly be wrung and possibly be broken... Wrap it carefully round with hobbies and little luxuries; avoid all entanglements; lock it up safe in the casket or coffin of your selfishness. But in that casket ... it will change. It will not be broken; it will become unbreakable, impenetrable, irredeemable.

The alternative to tragedy, or at least to the risk of tragedy, is damnation. The only place outside Heaven where you can be perfectly safe from all the dangers and perturbations of love is Hell.

≈ *THE FOUR LOVES*

To God,
WILHELM VON KAULBACH (1805–74)

Acknowledgements

The Editor and Publishers are grateful for permission to use the following
material, which is reproduced by permission of the copyright holders.

*The Four Loves, Letters to Malcolm, Chiefly on Prayer, Reflections on the Psalms,
Surprised by Joy,* and the essays 'The Efficacy of Prayer' and 'Equality' are
reproduced by kind permission of Harcourt Brace & Company.
*The Great Divorce, Mere Christianity, Miracles, The Problem of Pain, The Screwtape
Letters,* and the essay 'The Weight of Glory' are reproduced by kind
permission of HarperCollins*Publishers.*
The Pilgrim's Regress is reproduced by kind permission of
Wm. B. Eeerdmans Publishing Co.
They Stand Together is reproduced by kind permission of
Curtis Brown Pte Ltd.

All items are the copyright of C.S. Lewis Pte Ltd.

Full details of the writings of C.S.Lewis can be found in
C.S. Lewis: A Companion and Guide, by Walter Hooper,
published by HarperSanFrancisco in 1996.